Zakka
WOOL APPLIQUÉ

60+ Sweetly Stitched Designs
Useful Projects for Joyful Living

Minki Kim

stash BOOKS
an imprint of C&T Publishing

Text and photography copyright © 2020 by Minki Kim

Artwork copyright © 2020 by C&T Publishing, Inc.

Publisher: Amy Barret-Daffin

Creative Director: Gailen Runge

Acquisitions Editor: Roxane Cerda

Managing Editor: Liz Aneloski

Editor: Karla Menaugh

Technical Editor: Julie Waldman

Cover/Book Designer: April Mostek

Production Coordinator: Tim Manibusan

Production Editor: Jennifer Warren

Illustrator: Valyrie Gillum

Photo Assistant: Gregory Ligman

Cover photography by Minki Kim; photography by Minki Kim, unless otherwise noted

Published by Stash Books, an imprint of C&T Publishing, Inc., P.O. Box 1456, Lafayette, CA 94549

Library of Congress Cataloging-in-Publication Data

Names: Kim, Minki, 1973- author.

Title: Zakka wool appliqué : 60+ sweetly stitched designs, useful projects for joyful living / Minki Kim.

Description: Lafayette : C&T Publishing, [2020]

Identifiers: LCCN 2019042515 | ISBN 9781617459344 (trade paperback) | ISBN 9781617459351 (ebook)

Subjects: LCSH: Appliqué--Japan--Patterns. | Embroidery--Japan--Patterns. | Felt work. | Textile crafts--Japan.

Classification: LCC TT769.J3 K56 2020 | DDC 746.44/5041--dc23

LC record available at https://lccn.loc.gov/2019042515

Printed in China

10 9 8 7 6 5 4 3 2 1

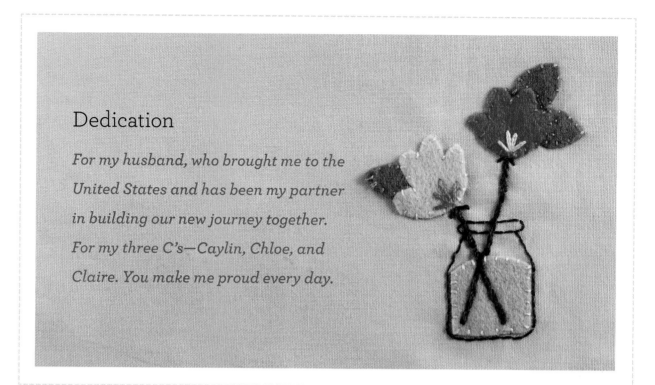

Dedication

For my husband, who brought me to the United States and has been my partner in building our new journey together. For my three C's—Caylin, Chloe, and Claire. You make me proud every day.

Acknowledgments

I am very grateful to all the following:

Amy Barrett-Daffin and Roxane Cerda, who always listen to my ideas and support my books from the beginning to the end. Karla Menaugh for helping me and making the book easy to read.

All my Riley Blake Designs family, Erin Sampson and Alex Veronelli from Aurifil threads, Taylored Expressions, LECIEN (COSMO Embroidery Floss), Alice from Alice Caroline fabrics, Lindsey Grand from The Warm Company, Sara SJ Kim from Dailylike Canada, Annie Unrein from ByAnnie, Yvonne Busdeker from OLFA Craft North America, and whaus.co.kr. I truly appreciate you for trusting me and supporting me without question.

My little Claire, who always plays around me, keeps me company, and loves everything Mom makes. And to my Chloe and Caylin, who share the most honest feedback that helps me try another and another.

My husband, Alex, for being my best pal.

Contents

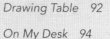

SPRING

Introduction

Drawing and designing are my favorite things to do, but my happiest moments are when I see my pencil drawings given new life as wall art in my kitchen corner, a pouch my friend uses every day, or a message board where my little girl sneakily puts her note for Mama.

I wrote two books about sewing illustrations, a technique that combines bits of appliqué with machine stitching. I found many sewists hesitate to use the sewing machine for embroidery, and hand embroidery has irresistible charm, of course. For me, wool felt was the perfect medium to transfer my love of raw-edge appliqué onto fabrics. Without any sketch, I cut a shape of a fried egg and stitched it onto fabric scraps. Then strawberry jam, a dog, two dogs … On each day, I was full of new ideas, and my wool-felt appliqué pile started to grow!

I had such a fun and productive winter while I was designing the appliqué patterns for this book. The best part of hand stitching is that you can be next your family watching television or listening to them play while your hands are busy with your needlework. With a basket of embroidery floss and wool felt scraps, you can draw anything, anywhere, until you get tired of stitching. But that didn't happen to me. I enjoyed stitching new designs on the various scraps of solid fabrics each day and the next day!

This book shows you six projects that you can make with your appliqué designs. In addition, I have included many more wool appliqué / embroidery patterns that you can adapt and create into new projects. If you love these ideas and want to make them with your quilting stash instead of wool felt, that works, too. See Gallery of Project Ideas (page 54) and Stitches and Patterns (page 72).

I hope to share my joy with you, and I hope these designs and project ideas bring happiness to your everyday life.

Downloadable Patterns

You can download and print any of the patterns at
tinyurl.com/11386-patterns-download. Make sure you print the images at 100%!

Basic Techniques

Materials

WOOL FELT

I used 100% wool felt for the appliqué designs in this book. I prefer 100% wool felt to traditional wool fabric because the colors are brighter. All the designs shown here are made with wool felt from Taylored Expressions.

THREAD

I used a variety of threads, such as Aurifil's 12-weight cotton/wool thread, Aurifil's Cotton Floss, and LECIEN's COSMO Embroidery Floss. The 12-weight thread is handy because you don't need to separate the strands. I mostly used a single strand or sometimes a double strand of the thread. The embroidery flosses are 6-stranded cotton flosses. For the embroidery floss, I used mostly 2 strands unless noted otherwise. A single strand of 12-weight thread is equal to 2 strands of floss.

SCISSORS

Save a pair of scissors for felt cutting only. The felt will dull your scissors, so it's better not to use your fabric scissors for felt cutting.

/ STORING TIP / I store my most frequently used felts and embroidery floss, a pair of felt scissors, a pair of thread scissors, a pincushion with needle, and some pins all together in one big sewing case.

When I am ready to sit down and start stitching, it's easy to bring out just that one case. When I have to leave for other chores, I can simply close the case and leave it ready for the next time I want to stitch!

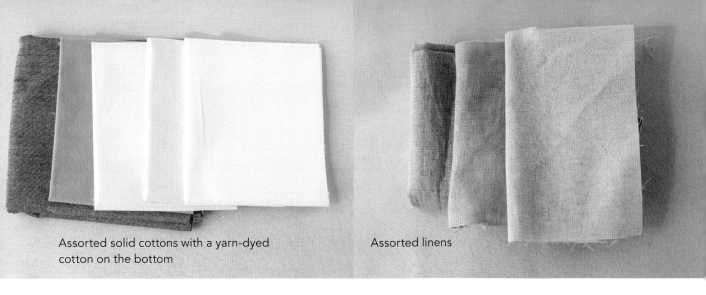

Assorted solid cottons with a yarn-dyed cotton on the bottom

Assorted linens

BACKGROUND FABRIC

A variety of linens and solid cottons went into these projects. If you choose linen, be sure to prewash it before you start stitching. Linen slightly shrinks, so it's better to have the shrinkage happen before you use it.

Transferring a Design to Fabric

WINDOW OR LIGHTBOX METHOD

One of the simplest methods is to make a photocopy of the design, tape it to a bright window, and trace the design onto your fabric. If you have a lightbox, tracing is even easier.

TABLET

Open a blank page on your tablet and set the screen brightness to the highest level. Place the pattern on top of the screen and hold it steady with your hand or use masking tape to lightly tape it to the tablet. Trace the pattern, taking care not to scratch the screen.

CUT OUT THE DESIGN

If your background fabric is dark, make a copy of the design and cut out each element. Place the paper elements on the fabric and use them as templates to trace the outline.

JUST DRAW!

You can draw right on the fabric. I highly recommend drawing because it adds your personal character to the design and you don't have to stress out about transferring all the lines perfectly. Most of the designs in this book will look good even if they are slightly different from the pattern, so let your own creativity shine through!

How to Attach Appliqué Pieces

FUSIBLE WEB

If there are many appliqué pieces in the design, use fusible web to attach the wool felt pieces to the background. Before you trace the design onto the fusible web, reverse the pattern so you can iron it onto the back of the wool felt piece.

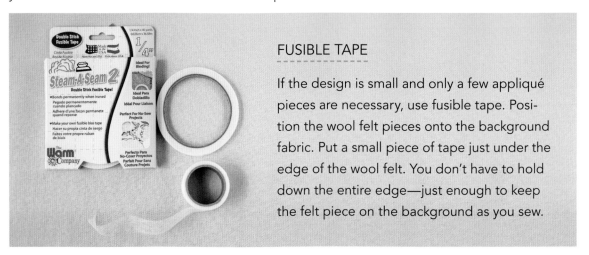

FUSIBLE TAPE

If the design is small and only a few appliqué pieces are necessary, use fusible tape. Position the wool felt pieces onto the background fabric. Put a small piece of tape just under the edge of the wool felt. You don't have to hold down the entire edge—just enough to keep the felt piece on the background as you sew.

PIN OR STAPLE

You can also use pins or staples to position the appliqué pieces. Make sure your finished projects will not be frequently washed if you use this method, because you have just the stitches to hold the appliqué to the background. Take out the staples after finishing the embroidery.

How to Appliqué

1. Transfer the design onto the background fabric using a temporary fabric pen. / **A**

2. Trace the appliqué design onto the paper side of the fusible web. *Be sure to reverse the design.* To print the patterns, see Downloadable Patterns (page 6). Roughly cut out each piece and fuse it onto the wool felt. / **B**

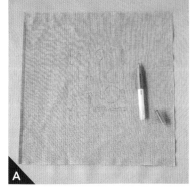

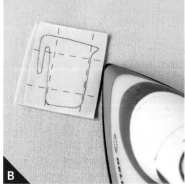

3. Cut out the wool felt shape on the traced line. Remove the paper backing. / C

4. Place the shape on the background fabric in the desired location and iron to fuse. / D

5. Using a matching-color thread, whipstitch the appliqué pieces to the background fabric. / E

6. Set the fabric into an embroidery hoop. Embroider the design as noted. *The number in parentheses on each stitch diagram indicates the number of strands of embroidery floss I used.* / F

/ TIP / If you want to make a wall art using a canvas, neatly fold the four edges of your stitched piece. Trim the excess fabric; then center the stitchery on the front of the canvas and staple the edges to the back.

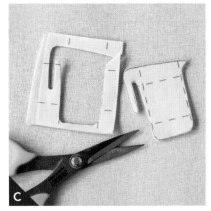

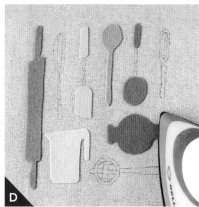

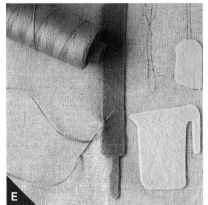

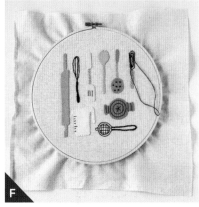

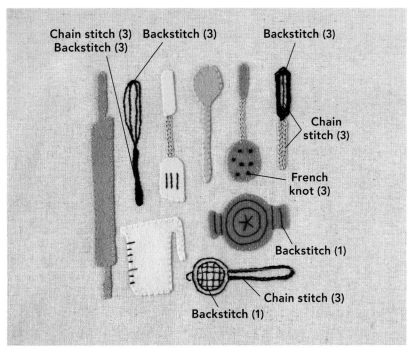

Chain stitch (3)
Backstitch (3)

Backstitch (3)

Backstitch (3)

Chain stitch (3)

French knot (3)

Backstitch (1)

Chain stitch (3)

Backstitch (1)

STITCH GUIDE

Backstitch

Chain Stitch

French Knot

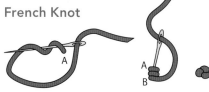

Lazy Daisy Stitch

Satin Stitch

Straight Stitch

Whipstitch

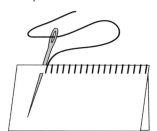

PROJECTS

Little Patch Coasters

Finished coaster: *6″ diameter*

Coasters are nice little projects to make in wool felt appliqué. With pretty fabric scraps, you can create a one-of-a-kind coaster easily and quickly. I made a round coaster, but you can change the shape and size depending on your preference. I added hand quilting for extra charm. I chose one strand of Aurifil's white 12-weight thread because most of the prints are busy. If your patchwork is calm, try colorful thread.

Materials and Supplies

Assorted felt scraps for appliqué pieces

Linen: *7″ × 7″ for appliqué background*

Fabric scraps for patchwork

Backing: *6½″ × 6½″ for coaster back*

Cotton batting: *7″ × 7″*

Thread: Neutral (ivory) and embroidery floss (white and colors to match your felt)

Cutting

Fabric scraps

See the patchwork assembly diagram (page 17).

A: *1½″ × 5½″*

B: *1½″ × 6″*

C: *2½″ × 6″*

D: *2½″ × ½″*

E: *2½″ × 2½″*

Instructions

Seam allowances are ¼˝ unless otherwise noted. See Basic Techniques (page 7) and Stitch Guide (page 12) for information on wool felt appliqué.

APPLIQUÉ AND STITCH THE DESIGN

1. Transfer the appliqué design onto the linen. You can use the Egg Fry pattern (page 80) or another pattern of your choice.

2. Prepare the wool appliqué cutouts and appliqué them onto the linen using the whipstitch and 2 strands of embroidery floss. Add any embroidery accents.

3. Trim the embroidered linen to 3¾˝ × 3½˝.

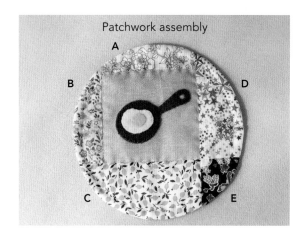

Patchwork assembly

SEW THE PATCHWORK

1. Place the appliqué on the batting, about 1¾˝ from the top and 2˝ from the left. / A

2. Place the print A rectangle on top of the linen, right sides together and matching the top raw edges. Stitch through all layers. Open and press the print outward. / B

3. Repeat to add the print B and C rectangles. / C-D

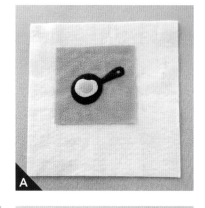

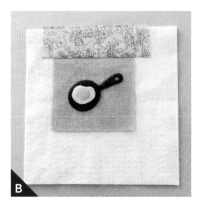

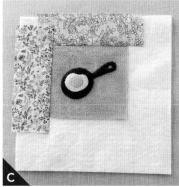

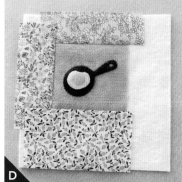

4. Sew the print D and E rectangles end to end and press the seam allowance toward print D. In the same manner as the previous rectangles, add the D/E strip to the right side of the coaster top. Open and press. / **E-F**

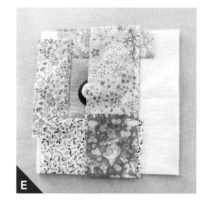
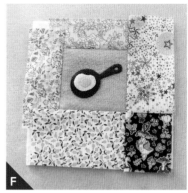

5. Using a temporary fabric pen, draw a 6˝ circle (next page) on the backing fabric. Place the coaster top and back right sides together, taking care to center the circle over the stitched design. Stitch together on the drawn line, leaving a gap for turning. Trim the excess batting with scissors. / **G**

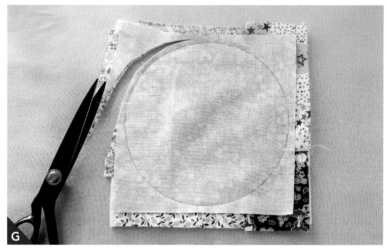

6. Turn right side out and press. Hand stitch the gap closed. Hand quilt along the patchwork. Topstitch around the edge of the coaster by hand, using 2 strands of embroidery floss, or by machine.

/ TIP / **When topstitching by hand, pull the thread just a little. This creates nice wrinkles that add handmade charm.**

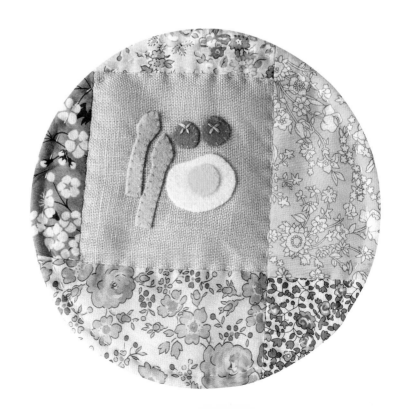

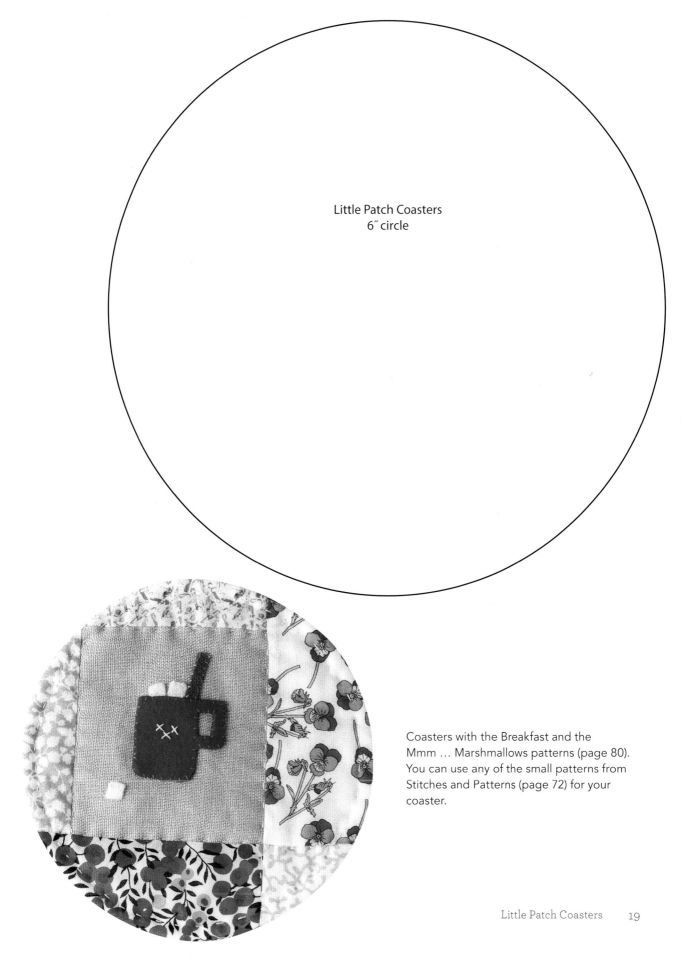

Little Patch Coasters
6″ circle

Coasters with the Breakfast and the Mmm … Marshmallows patterns (page 80). You can use any of the small patterns from Stitches and Patterns (page 72) for your coaster.

Pocket Pencil Case

Finished case: 7½″ wide × 4″ high × 4″ deep

A maker can never have enough pencil cases! I have made many different styles of pencil cases, but I have very few left because a pencil case is the best gift for any occasion.

This roomy pencil case with a stitched pocket can hold almost all you need on the go. The instructions are simple since we quilt the exterior and the lining together. Choose any of the designs in this book depending on how your pencil case is going to be used—a sewing theme for a sewist, a cooking theme for a baker, or a nature theme for your gardener friend!

Materials and Supplies

Assorted wool felt scraps for appliqué pieces

Off-white fabric: 5½″ × 10″ for appliqué background

Print 1: Fat quarter (18″ × 21″) for case body

Print 2: At least 4½″ × 12″ for case bottom

Print 3: ½ yard for zipper binding and lining

Cotton batting: 13″ × 16″

Fusible interfacing: 3″ × 7½″

13″ zipper or longer (A longer zipper is preferred.)

Embroidery thread: Black, red, gray, and colors to match your wool felt

Cutting

For the case body, see the pattern (pages 26 and 27).

Print 1

• 2 case bodies

Print 2

• 1 case bottom 4½″ × 12″

Print 3

• 1 pocket lining 3½″ × 8″

• 2 zipper bindings 2½″ × 12″

• 1 case lining 14″ × 17″

• 6 binding strips 1½″ × 5″

Instructions

Seam allowances are ¼″ unless otherwise noted. See Basic Techniques (page 7) and Stitch Guide (page 12) for information on wool felt appliqué.

APPLIQUÉ AND STITCH THE DESIGN

1. Transfer the appliqué design onto the off-white fabric. You can use the On My Desk pattern (page 94) or another pattern of your choice.

2. Prepare the wool appliqué cutouts and arrange them on the traced design. Fuse the wool felt pieces to the background fabric. Sketch in or trace the remaining design with a temporary marking pen.

3. Appliqué the wool felt pieces to the background. See the embroidery guide for the stitches and number of strands to use for the embroidery elements. / A

4. Trim the appliquéd fabric to 3½″ × 8″.

MAKE THE POCKET

1. Center the interfacing piece 3″ × 7½″ on the wrong side of the print 3 pocket lining and fuse it in place.

2. Right sides together, sew the lining to the appliquéd pocket along the top edge. Refold the pocket and lining wrong sides together and press. / B

3. Pin the pocket to the print 1 case body, aligning at the bottom short edges. Right sides together, center and place the print 2 case bottom on the bottom edge of the pocket, matching the raw edges. Pin in place and stitch the pieces together. / C

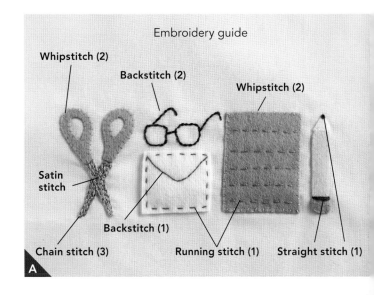

Embroidery guide

Whipstitch (2)

Backstitch (2)

Whipstitch (2)

Satin stitch

Backstitch (1)

Chain stitch (3)

Running stitch (1)

Straight stitch (1)

A

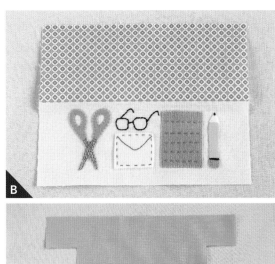

B

C

4. Center the remaining print 1 case body on the other side of the case bottom. Pin in place and sew together. Press the seam allowances toward the case body. / D

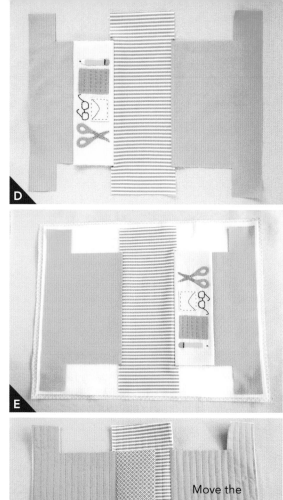

5. Place the print 3 case lining on your table with the wrong side up. Center the batting on top. Place the pieced case body on top, right side up. Make sure the appliqué pocket is on the case body side. / E

6. Quilt as desired, folding the pocket out of the way as you quilt each section. I sewed straight lines ½˝ apart using matching-color threads. Trim the excess batting and lining. / F & G

SEW THE ZIPPER

1. Fold both 12˝ zipper-binding strips in half lengthwise, wrong sides together. Press.

2. Pin the binding strips to the exterior, aligning the raw edges. Sew to the exterior.

Move the pocket out of the way as you quilt.

3. Press the folded edge of the bindings toward the lining; glue baste. Machine stitch just to the right of the binding seam. / H

4. Place one side of the zipper right side up, with the zipper teeth aligned right under the binding edge at one end of the case body and the top of the zipper ⅜˝ from the raw edge. Pin in place and machine stitch right under the binding edge. Let the extra length hang off the other edge for now.

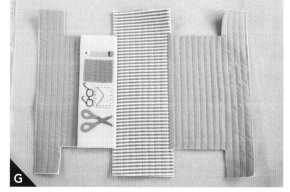

5. Open the zipper and repeat Step 4 to attach the zipper to the other end of the case body. / I

/ TIP / A longer zipper is easier to attach.

ASSEMBLE THE CASE

1. Turn the case inside out. On each side, fold at the inside corners and match the raw edges, aligning the seam at the end of the zipper with the center of the pouch bottom.

2. Stitch across the raw edges. If your zipper had extra length, trim it even with the raw edges. Place a binding strip on top of a zipper side, aligning the long raw edges. Stitch across, backstitching at the beginning and end to secure. Fold in the raw edge and pin to the other side of the seam. Topstitch to finish the edge. / J

3. Repeat for the other side. / K

4. Now the case has 4 openings that will be sewn up to create the sides. Starting on one of the front corners, mark the center of the folded edge of the cutout square. Open the cutout and flatten it, bringing the raw edges of the cutout square together so the mark at the fold meets the side seam. Pin together along this edge, catching the side of the pocket in your pinning. Wrong side up, center and align a binding strip with the raw edges of the case. Fold in both short ends of the binding strip and pin. Stitch across the raw edges, backstitching at the beginning and end to secure. / L

5. Fold in the long raw edge of the binding strip and pin to the other side of the seam. Topstitch to finish the edge.

6. Repeat the process to finish the other 3 corners of the case. The 2 back corners will not have the pocket included in the seam.

7. Turn right side out and press into shape. / M

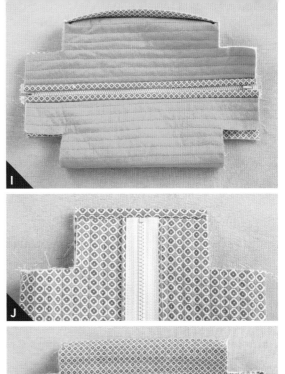

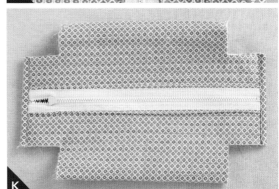

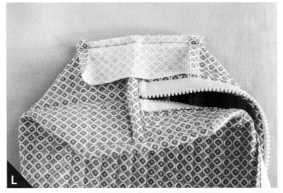

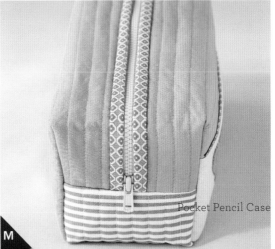

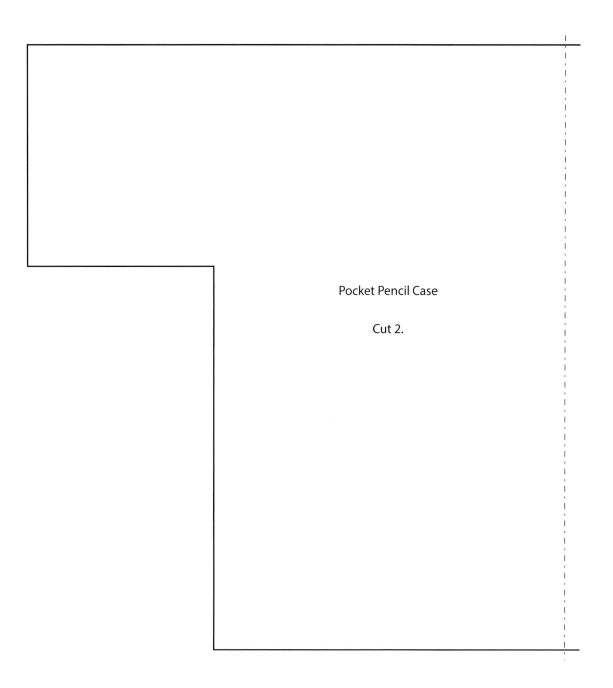

Pocket Pencil Case

Cut 2.

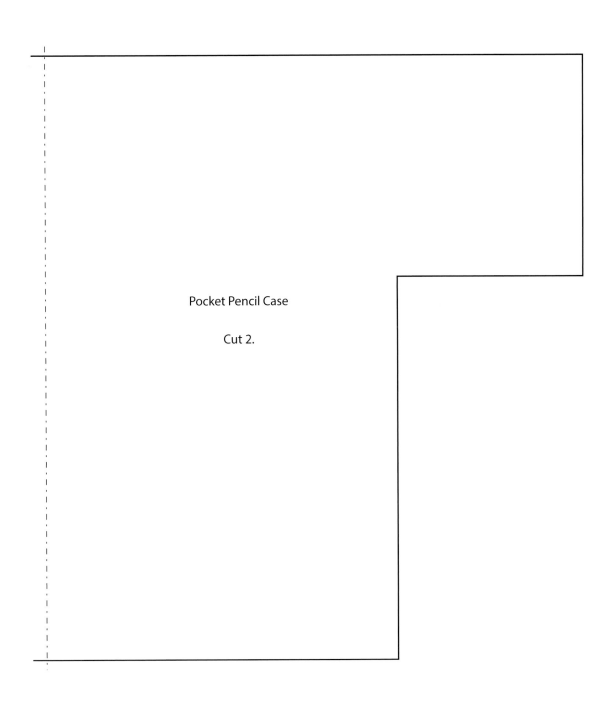

Pocket Pencil Case

Cut 2.

Boxy Sewing Case

Finished case: 7˝ wide × 7˝ high × 4½˝ deep

I have always loved making the boxy-style zipper pouch because it can stand by itself and the front is a nice little canvas on which to draw wool-felt appliqué designs. This sewing case is roomy enough to hold your usual sewing items.

Materials and Supplies

Assorted wool felt scraps for appliqué pieces

Linen: 9˝ × 9˝ for case front

Print 1: 7½˝ × 7½˝ for case back

Print 2: Fat quarter (18˝ × 21˝) for case side

Lining: ½ yard

Medium-weight fusible batting: ½ yard

20˝-wide woven fusible interfacing: 1 yard (I like Pellon's SF101 Shape-Flex.)

14½˝ zipper or longer

Cotton ribbon: ½˝ × 4˝ long

Embroidery thread: Black and colors to match your wool felt

Cutting

For the pouch lining and batting, see the pattern (pages 34 and 35).

Print 2

• 1 case bottom 5˝ × 14½˝

• 2 zipper sides 2½˝ × 14½˝

Lining

• 1 case body

Medium-weight fusible batting

• 1 case body

Woven fusible interfacing

• 2 squares 7½˝ × 7½˝

• 1 case body

Cotton ribbon

• 2 lengths ½˝ × 2˝

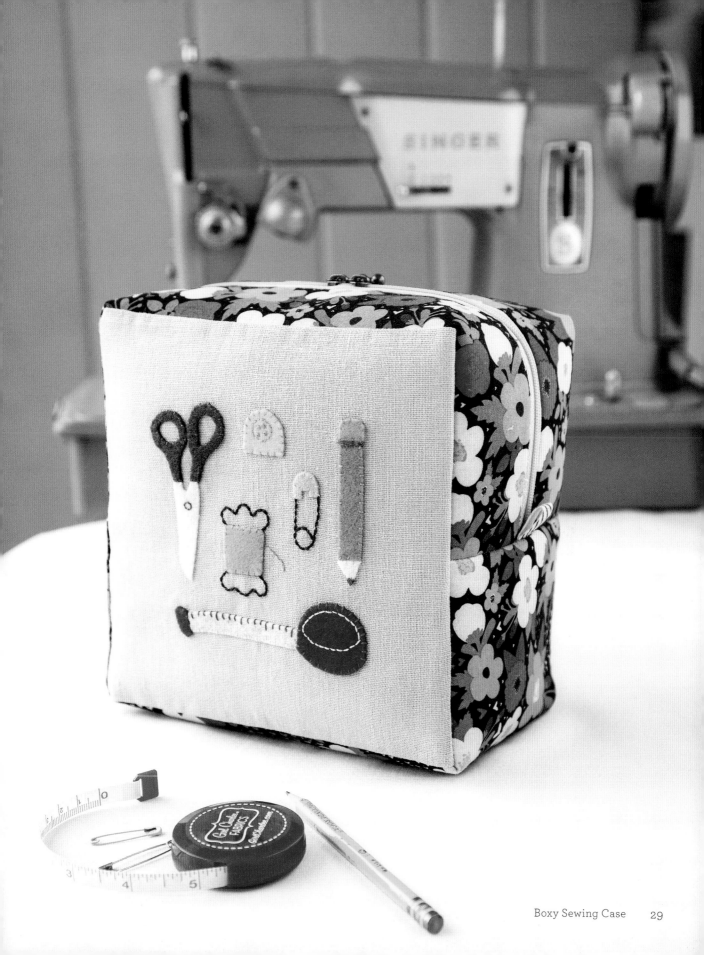

Instructions

Seam allowances are ¼″ unless otherwise noted. See Basic Techniques (page 7) and Stitch Guide (page 12) for information on wool felt appliqué.

APPLIQUÉ AND STITCH THE DESIGN

1. Press to adhere the woven fusible interfacing squares to the wrong side of the linen case front and the print 1 case back.

2. Transfer the appliqué design onto the linen. You can use the Sewing Day pattern (page 96) or another pattern of your choice.

3. Prepare the wool appliqué cutouts; arrange them on the traced design. Fuse the pieces to the linen. Sketch in or trace the remaining design with a temporary marking pen.

4. Appliqué the wool felt pieces to the linen. See the embroidery guide for the stitches and number of strands to use for the embroidery elements. / A

5. Trim the appliquéd linen to 7½″ × 7½″. Mark the center of the top and bottom by lightly folding the edges in half.

MAKE THE OUTSIDE

1. Center a print 2 zipper side on the top of the linen, right sides together. Pin and sew. Center the print 2 case bottom on the bottom edge of the linen. Pin and sew. / B

2. Sew the case back and the remaining print 2 zipper side as shown. Press the seams toward the square fabrics. / C

3. Center and press the fusible batting on the wrong side of the case body. / D

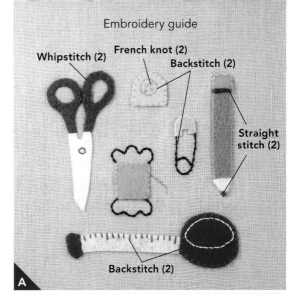

Embroidery guide

Whipstitch (2) French knot (2) Backstitch (2)

Straight stitch (2)

Backstitch (2)

A

B

C

D

SEW THE ZIPPER

1. Place the zipper facedown on top of the right side of a print 2 zipper side. You will be able to see the wrong side of the zipper. Pin the zipper in place. Sew the zipper and fabric together using a zipper foot, stitching close to the zipper-tape edge. Backstitch to secure. / **E**

2. Repeat Step 1 on the other side of the case to create a tube with the inside out.

SEW THE SIDES

1. Open the zipper halfway. With right sides together, rearrange the pieces so that the zipper is aligned at the center of the case bottom. Pin right sides together. Fold a 2″ ribbon in half and insert the folded edge between the 2 pieces of fabric, centered over the zipper, to make a tab. The loop will be between the right sides of fabric, and the raw edges should be aligned with the raw edges of the case. Pin in place and sew together. / **F**

2. Repeat Step 1 on the opposite end of the zipper.

3. Now the case has 4 openings that will be sewn up to create the sides. Starting on any side, mark the center of the folded edge of the cutout square. Open the cutout and flatten it, bringing the raw edges of the cut-out square together so the mark at the fold meets the side seam. Sew together along this edge. Backstitch at the beginning and end of the seam to secure.

4. Repeat Step 3 on the 3 remaining sides. / **G**

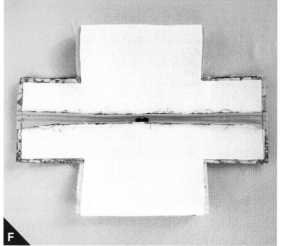

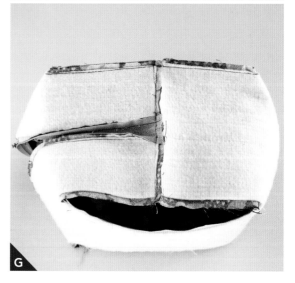

MAKE THE LINING

1. Fuse the case-body interfacing to the wrong side of the lining fabric. Press each long end of the lining fabric ¼″ toward the wrong side.

2. Place the lining piece right side up. With right sides together, match the corners of the 2 ends to the corners of the side tabs. Pin and sew with a ⅜″ seam for a nice fit, making sure to backstitch at the beginning and end of the seam. Repeat on the opposite side.

3. Follow Sew the Sides, Step 3 (previous page) to finish the lining sides, but use a ⅜″ seam for a nice fit. Turn the lining right side out. / H

FINISH IT UP

Slip the outside pouch into the lining, wrong sides together. Pin the lining to the zipper, folding the raw edge to the inside, and hand stitch in place. Turn the pouch right side out. Press along the sides and bottom. / I

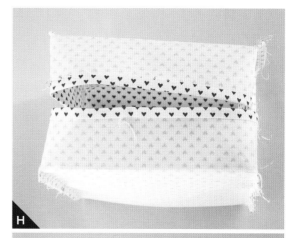

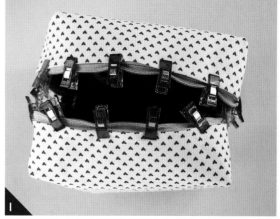

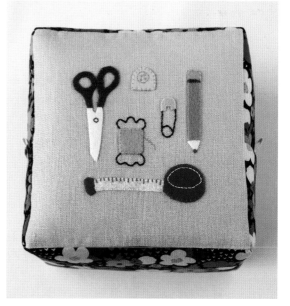

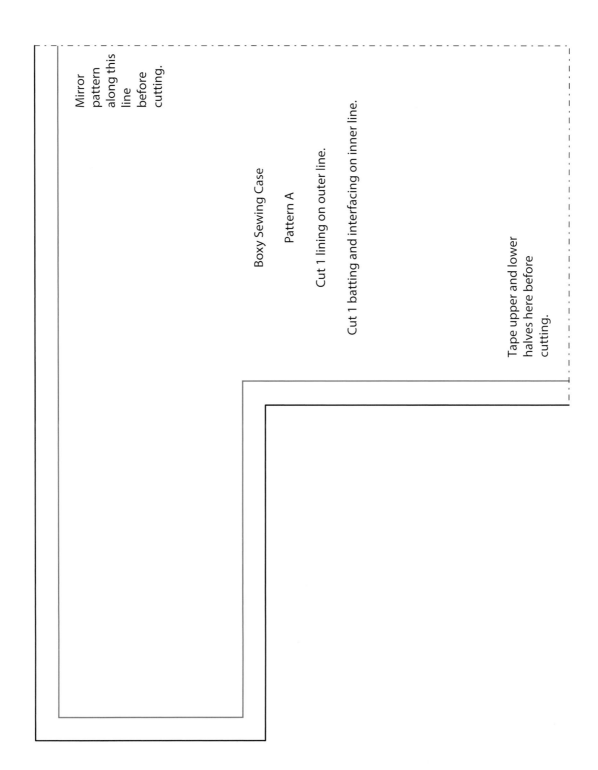

Mirror pattern along this line before cutting.

Boxy Sewing Case

Pattern A

Cut 1 lining on outer line.

Cut 1 batting and interfacing on inner line.

Tape upper and lower halves here before cutting.

Trace or copy patterns A and B and tape them together. Tape together 2 more pieces of blank paper and trace the reversed A/B unit onto them. Tape the 2 traced patterns together at the center to make a full template.

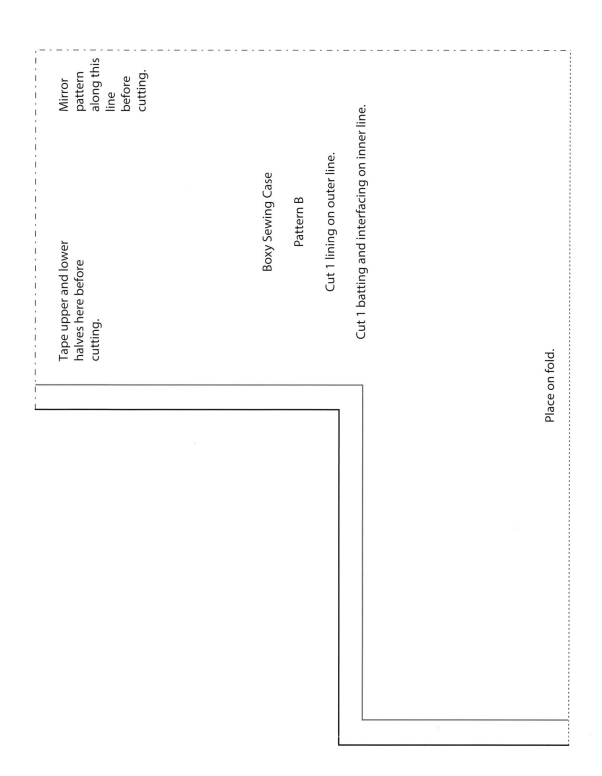

Mirror pattern along this line before cutting.

Tape upper and lower halves here before cutting.

Boxy Sewing Case

Pattern B

Cut 1 lining on outer line.

Cut 1 batting and interfacing on inner line.

Place on fold.

Sewing Time Pocket Folder

Finished folder: 10½″ × 10″

Big pocket folders are another good way to show off your appliqué with a finished project that is very useful. Two big vinyl pockets make it easy to find small materials and store templates safely. Adjust the case size depending on the zipper size you have on hand or the appliqué designs you prefer.

Materials and Supplies

Assorted wool felt scraps for appliqué pieces

Off-white solid cotton: 12″ × 12″ for front cover

Print 1: 10″ × 10″ for folder back

Print 2: ¼ yard for folder side and binding

Print 3: ⅔ yard for lining

Clear vinyl: 10″ × 17″ (I like Premium Clear Vinyl by C&T Publishing or ByAnnie.com.)

Medium-weight fusible fleece: ⅓ yard (I like Fusible Iron-On Fleece [4 ounces] from Dailylike Canada or Pellon's 987F Fusible Fleece.)

20″-wide woven fusible interfacing: ⅔ yard (I like Pellon's SF101 Shape-Flex.)

9″ zippers: 2

Fusible web: 10″ × 10″

Embroidery floss: Dark brown and colors to match your felt

Cutting

Print 2

• 1 folder side 2″ × 10″

• 2 binding strips 2½″ × width of fabric

Print 3

• 1 lining 10″ × 21″

• 1 lining center 2″ × 10″

• 2 vinyl bindings 2″ × 10″

• 4 zipper bindings 2″ × 10″

• 4 zipper-end tabs 1½″ × 3″

Clear vinyl

• 2 pockets 8¼″ × 10″

Medium-weight fusible fleece

• 1 rectangle 10″ × 21″

Woven fusible interfacing

• 1 folder front 10″ × 10″

• 1 folder back 10″ × 10″

Instructions

Seam allowances are ¼″ unless otherwise noted. See Basic Techniques (page 7) and Stitch Guide (page 12) for information on wool felt appliqué.

APPLIQUÉ AND STITCH THE DESIGN

1. Press to adhere the woven fusible interfacing squares to the wrong side of the off-white front cover and the print 1 folder back.

2. Transfer the appliqué design onto the off-white fabric. You can use the Sew Happy pattern (page 91) or another pattern of your choice.

3. Prepare the wool appliqué cutouts and arrange them on the traced design. Fuse the wool felt pieces to the background. Sketch in or trace the remaining design with a temporary marking pen.

4. Appliqué the wool cutouts to the background. See the embroidery guide for the stitches and number of strands to use for the embroidery elements. / A

5. Trim the appliquéd fabric to 10″ × 10″.

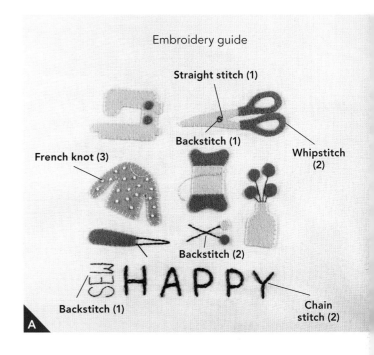

Embroidery guide

Straight stitch (1)
Backstitch (1)
Whipstitch (2)
French knot (3)
Backstitch (2)
Backstitch (1)
Chain stitch (2)

A

MAKE THE CASE EXTERIOR

1. Sew the print 2 folder side 2″ × 10″ between the appliquéd folder front and print 1 folder back, aligning the long edges. Press the seam allowances toward the center. The folder exterior should measure 21″ × 10″.

2. Attach the fusible fleece to the wrong side of the folder exterior. / B

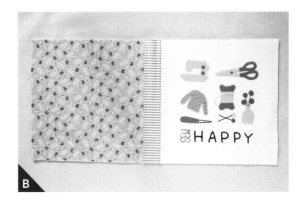

B

MAKE THE VINYL POCKETS

1. Fold the zipper-end tabs 1½″ × 3″ in half, wrong sides together. Fold both edges ¼″ toward the inside and press. Slip a zipper end into each tab and topstitch about ¹⁄₁₆″ from the folded edge. / C

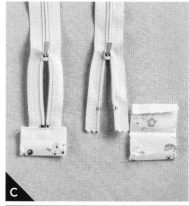

2. Sandwich the zipper between 2 print 3 zipper-binding strips 2″ × 10″, right sides together. Pin and sew with a ¼″ seam allowance. Reposition the fabrics with wrong sides together and press. Repeat Steps 1 and 2 to prepare the second zipper. / D

3. Fold the print 3 vinyl-binding strips 2″ × 10″ in half lengthwise, wrong sides together; press. Unfold. Bring the long raw edges toward the center crease on the wrong side and press. Fold in half again and press.

4. Slide the long edge of the vinyl pocket into a binding strip. Sew the binding to the vinyl pocket ¹⁄₁₆″ from the outer edge. Repeat to attach a binding strip to the second vinyl pocket. / E

/ TIP / Place a scrap of fabric under the vinyl to keep it from sticking to the sewing machine.

5. Change to a zipper foot. Sew the vinyl-binding piece to the other side of the zipper tape along the top edge of the binding. Repeat to attach the other vinyl pocket to the remaining zipper. / F

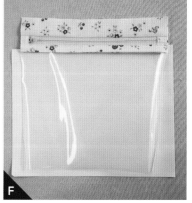

6. Sew the print 3 lining center 2″ × 10″ between the 2 pocket units.

ASSEMBLE THE CASE

1. Place the folder exterior wrong side up. Place the lining right side up on top of the folder exterior.

2. With the zippers closed, place the vinyl pocket unit right side up on top of the lining and exterior. The zipper pulls should be at the top edge. Use binding clips to hold all the layers in place.

3. Stitch along the vertical edges of the print 3 lining center to form the inner edge of the pockets. / G

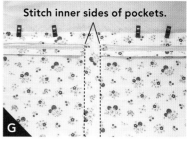

Stitch inner sides of pockets.

ATTACH THE BINDING

1. Sew the print 2 binding strips together with a diagonal seam. Trim the seam allowance to ¼″. Press the seam open. / H

2. Fold the binding strip in half lengthwise, wrong sides together, and press. / I

3. Lining up the raw edges, sew the binding to the lining side of the case, mitering the corners as you go. Start sewing a few inches away from a corner and leave the first few inches of binding unsewn. Stop sewing ¼″ from the corner and backstitch to secure. / J

4. Lift the needle and presser foot and rotate the case to the left. Fold the binding up at the corner to form a 45° angle; then fold it straight down along the second side of the case. Stitch this side, ending ¼″ from the corner as before. Repeat this step on the remaining 2 sides. / K-L

5. Follow Step 4 to form the last corner. Stop stitching a few inches from where you began on the first side. Fold the ending tail of the binding back where it meets the beginning tail, and measure 2½″. Cut the ending tail at this point. / M

6. Open both binding tails. Arrange them right sides together and forming a right angle. Pin in place and mark a diagonal line from corner to corner. Stitch on this line. Before trimming the seam allowance, check to make sure the seam has been sewn correctly and that the binding fits the quilt. / N

/ TIP / Make sure not to sew over the metal ends of the zipper when you sew the binding.

7. Trim the seam allowance on the binding join to ¼″ and press open. Refold the binding strip and stitch this last section to the case. / O

8. Fold the edge of the binding strip to the outside of the case. Hand stitch along the inside folded edge of the binding. / P

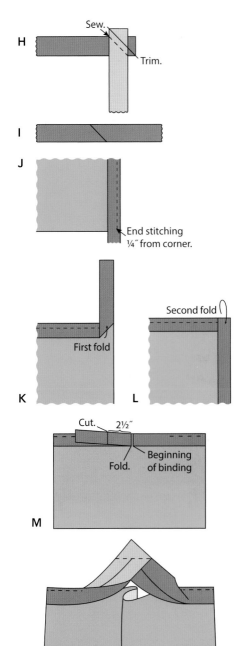

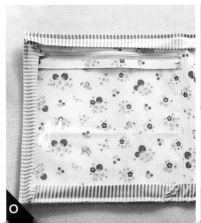

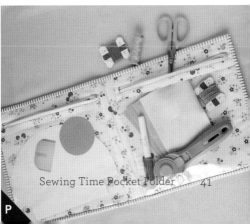

Jardin Pillow

Finished pillow: 21″ × 21″

For this pillow, I sewed together strips of pretty prints from my previous projects. When you pick the fabric colors, choose from your appliqué colors. Add coordinating accent colors for more fun.

Materials and Supplies

Assorted wool felt scraps for appliqué pieces

Linen: Fat quarter (18″ × 21″) for appliqué background

5 assorted prints: See Cutting (page 44) for the patchwork.

Lining: ⅔ yard for quilted pillow front

Binding A: 2½″ × width of fabric

Binding B: 2½″ × width of fabric

Backing: ⅔ yard for pillow

Cotton batting: 23″ × 23″

Embroidery floss: Dark brown and colors to match your felt

Cutting

Linen

• 1 appliqué background 13″ × 13″

5 assorted prints

Make a template from the triangle pattern (page 47). See the construction diagram (at right).

• Print A: 2½″ × 11″

• Print B: 3″ × 12″

• Print C: 2″ × 13″

• Print D: 1¼″ × 13″

• Print E1: 3 triangles

• Print E2: 4 triangles

• Print F: 3¼″ × 17½″

• Print G: 3″ × 17″

• Print H: 2¾″ × 20″

• Print I: 3¼″ × 20″

• Print J: 2½″ × 22″

Lining

• 1 square 24″ × 24″

Backing

• 2 pillow backs 16″ × 21″

Construction diagram

Instructions

Seam allowances are ¼″ unless otherwise noted. See Basic Techniques (page 7) and Stitch Guide (page 12) for information on wool felt appliqué.

APPLIQUÉ AND STITCH THE DESIGN

1. Transfer the appliqué design onto the linen. You can use the Windblown Bouquet pattern (page 116) or another pattern of your choice.

2. Prepare the wool appliqué cutouts and arrange them on the traced design. Fuse the wool felt pieces to the linen. Sketch in or trace the remaining design with a temporary marking pen.

3. Using 3 strands of embroidery thread, hand stitch each element to the linen. See the embroidery guide for the stitches and number of strands to use for the embroidery elements. **/ A**

4. Trim the appliquéd linen to 10″ × 11″.

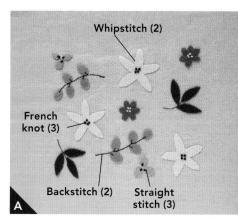

Embroidery guide

SEW THE PATCHWORK

1. Attach the patchwork strips in Log Cabin fashion. Start by sewing the print A rectangle to the left side of the appliqué rectangle. / **B**

2. Continue to add rectangles in a clockwise order—next the print B rectangle to the top and then the print C and D rectangles to the right side. / **C**

3. For the triangles at the bottom of the first round of patchwork, sew together 4 pink triangles and 3 light print triangles. Trim the strip to 4¼″ × 14¼″ and attach the strip to the bottom of the embroidered rectangle. / **D-G**

4. Sew the print G rectangle to the top of the patchwork, then the print H and print I rectangles to each side. Sew the print J rectangle to the bottom to complete the pillow top.

QUILT THE PILLOW TOP

1. Center and baste the pillow top, right side up, to the batting and the lining, right side down, using your preferred method. Quilt as desired. I quilted around each appliqué element, about ¼˝ from the edge. Around the outer edge of the appliquéd square and in the patchwork, I quilted straight lines ½˝ apart, parallel to the patchwork lines. / H

2. Trim off any excess batting and backing. Keeping the design centered, trim to 21˝ × 21˝.

MAKE THE PILLOW BACK

Fold one of the long edges of a backing fabric rectangle ½˝ to the wrong side. Press. Fold over another 1½˝ to the wrong side and press again. Topstitch along the edge of both folds and add straight lines ½˝ apart to give the edge extra strength. Repeat with the remaining pillow back.

/ TIP / If you are using a directional print, make sure the backing pieces are aligned in the right direction before sewing the pillow back.

ASSEMBLE THE PILLOW

1. Place the quilted pillow front on a flat surface, right side down. Matching up the raw edges at the top of the pillow, place one backing rectangle faceup so the wrong sides of the back and front are together. The folded edge should run across the center of the pillow. Place the second backing rectangle faceup with the raw edges aligned with the bottom of the pillow top. The folded backing edges will overlap at the center. Pin or sew ⅛˝ from the outside edges to secure.

2. Join the 2½˝ binding strips end to end with a diagonal seam. Trim the seam allowance to ¼˝ and press it open. Fold the binding strip in half, wrong sides together and long edges matching, and press.

3. Raw edges matching, start pinning the binding about 2″ above the lower left corner, where the corner patchwork meets. Stitch the binding to the edge of the pillow front, mitering the corners as you go. / I

4. Turn the binding over and stitch the folded edge to the back of the pillow. You can do this step by hand or machine.

/ TIP / For machine-finished binding, attach the binding to the front in the usual way. Fold the binding to the back and glue baste it in place, making sure it covers the previous seamline by at least ⅛″. Turn the piece to the front and stitch right under the binding through all the layers. It will catch the binding folded over to the back, but from the front.

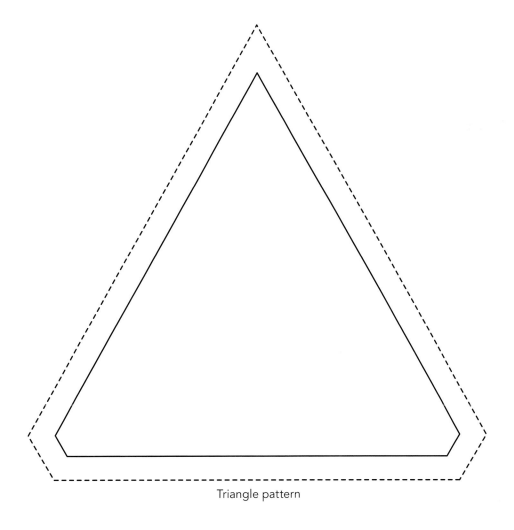

Triangle pattern

Floral Handbag

Finished bag: 11″ wide × 9″ high × 3″ deep (plus handles)

With a zippered pocket inside, this is a stylish and practical date bag!
Once you know the bag assembly, you can make it modern or classic by
changing the fabric or appliqué patterns. Leather handles can be easily found
online. Change to fabric handles or cotton webbing if you prefer.

Materials and Supplies

Assorted wool felt for appliqué

Yarn-dyed cotton: ½ yard for appliqué
background and binding

Print 1: Fat quarter (18″ × 21″) for back

Print 2: Fat quarter (18″ × 21″) for gusset

Lining: ½ yard

Medium-weight fusible fleece: 1 yard
(I like Fusible Iron-On Fleece [4 ounces] from
Dailylike Canada or Pellon's 987F Fusible Fleece.)

Woven fusible interfacing: 1 yard (I like Pellon's
SF101 Shape-Flex.)

Fusible interfacing: 1 yard (I like Pellon's
931TD Fusible Midweight.)

7″ zipper or longer

Magnetic snap: 1 set

Leather handles: 1 set 15½″ (I got mine from
whaus.co.kr or byhandsusa.com.)

Embroidery floss in colors to match your felt

Heavyweight thread, such as hand quilting
thread, for handle attachment

Cutting

Yarn-dyed cotton

- 1 appliqué background 13″ × 11″
- 1 binding strip 2″ × width of fabric

Print 1

- 1 bag back 11½″ × 9¼″

Print 2

- 2 side-gusset strips 3½″ × 14¾″

Lining

- 2 zipper-pocket rectangles 7¼″ × 11½″
- 2 zipper-pocket strips 2½″ × 11½″
- 1 bag lining 9¼″ × 11½″
- 1 pocket lining 9¼″ × 11½″
- 2 zipper-end tabs 1½″ × 5″
- 1 gusset 3½″ × 29″

Medium-weight fusible fleece (for exterior)

- 2 rectangles 9″ × 10½″. Using a spool as a template, round off the bottom corners.
- 2 strips 3″ × 14¼″

Woven fusible interfacing (for exterior)

- 2 rectangles 9¼″ × 11½″
- 2 rectangles 3½″ × 14½″

Fusible interfacing (for lining)

- 2 rectangles 9¼″ × 11½″
- 2 strips 3½″ × 14½″

Instructions

Seam allowances are ¼″ unless otherwise noted. See Basic Techniques (page 7) and Stitch Guide (page 12) for information on wool felt appliqué.

APPLIQUÉ AND STITCH THE DESIGN

1. Press to adhere the woven fusible interfacing to the wrong side of the appliqué front, print 1 back, and both print 2 side-gusset strips.

2. Transfer the appliqué design onto the yarn-dyed cotton. You can use the Dogwood in Bloom pattern (page 112) or another pattern of your choice.

3. Prepare the wool appliqué cutouts and arrange them on the traced design. Fuse the wool felt pieces to the yarn-dyed cotton. Sketch in or trace the remaining design with a temporary marking pen.

4. Using 2 strands of embroidery thread, hand stitch each element to the background. Be sure to clean up the excess thread on the back of the appliqué so it doesn't show through. See

the embroidery guide for the stitches and number of strands to use for the embroidery elements. / A

5. Trim the appliquéd fabric to 11½″ × 9¼″. This will be the front of the bag.

PREPARE THE BAG EXTERIOR

1. Sew the print 2 strips together end to end and press the seam open. This is the side gusset. / B

2. Press to adhere the fusible fleece to the wrong side of the bag front and bag back, matching the top raw edges. Leave ¼″ around bottom and sides without fleece.

3. Trim off the rounded bottom corners of the exterior front and back pieces, leaving ¼″ seam allowances.

ASSEMBLE THE BAG

1. Mark the bottom center of the bag front. Matching the center with the seamline of the gusset, pin them right sides together. Continue pinning around the curved corners and up the sides of the bag front. The gusset will extend a bit past the top edge of the front on both sides.

2. Remove the extension table of your sewing machine if you can. This will help you rotate the bag around the machine as you sew.

3. Lay the bag on your sewing machine with the gusset on top and the bag front on the bottom. Start sewing from the bag opening and slow down when you sew the round side. Clip the round corner seam for easy sewing. One stitch at a time and with the needle down, rotate your bag to finish the seam. / C-D

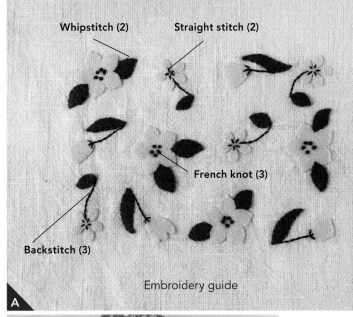

Whipstitch (2) Straight stitch (2)

French knot (3)

Backstitch (3)

Embroidery guide

A

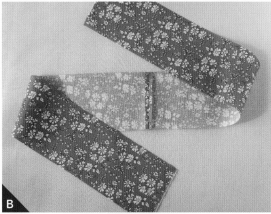

B

C

D

4. In the same manner, pin the bag back to the other side of the gusset and finish sewing the bag exterior. Trim the excess gusset. / **E-F**

MAKE THE ZIPPER POCKET

1. Fold the zipper-end tabs in half, wrong sides together. Fold both edges ¼˝ toward the inside and press. Slide a zipper end into each tab and topstitch about ¹⁄₁₆˝ from the folded edge.

2. Mark the center of the zipper and the center of the pocket piece. / **G**

3. Lay one zipper-pocket rectangle right side up. Place the zipper on top, wrong side up, matching the top raw edges. Place the other zipper-pocket rectangle, wrong side up, on top of the zipper. Pin and use a zipper foot to sew through all layers. / **H**

/ TIP / If you are not used to sewing two layers at once, sew one zipper-pocket rectangle to the zipper at a time.

4. Reposition the fabrics wrong sides together and press.

5. In the same manner, sew the 2 zipper-pocket strips to the other side of the zipper tape.

6. Pin together the zipper pocket unit from Step 5 and the pocket lining, both right sides up. Trim the excess zipper tab. Stitch around the raw edges with a ⅛˝ seam allowance, just to secure the pocket. / **I**

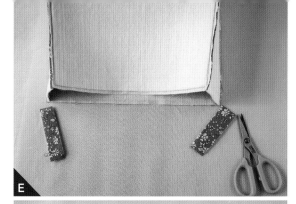

E

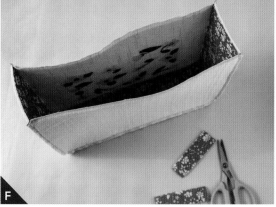

F

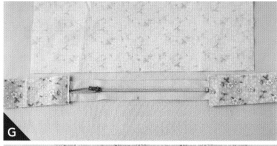

G

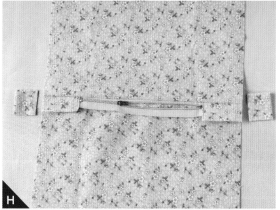

H

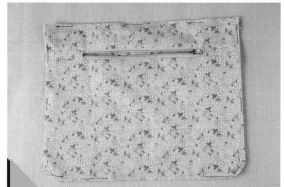

I

FINISH THE LINING

Following Assemble the Bag (page 51), sew the lining gusset to the zipper-pocket lining and the remaining lining piece. / J

ADD THE MAGNETIC SNAP

1. Mark the center of the front and back lining.

2. Following the manufacturer's guide, attach the magnetic snap. / K

ASSEMBLE THE BINDING

1. Put the lining inside the bag, wrong sides together, and pin in place around the top edge. Trim the lining if necessary.

2. Fold the binding strip in half lengthwise, wrong sides together, and press. Re-pin to attach the binding strip to the top of the bag/lining assembly, matching the raw edges of the bag. Sew all the way around.

3. Fold the binding to the inside and hand stitch it to the bag lining. / L

ADD THE HANDLES

Mark the handle placement 3˝ from each side of the bag. Using matching or contrasting heavyweight thread, cross-stitch the leather handles in place on each outer panel to finish, making sure that they sit opposite of each other. Press the bag well into shape. / M-N

Gallery of Project Ideas

Blossom boxy pouch,
6˝ wide × 6˝ high × 4˝ deep
(page 110)

Best Utensils wall art, 8″ × 10″ (page 74)

A Place for You pot holder with pocket, 8¼″ × 9½″ (page 80)

Floral Vine drawstring bag,
7½" wide × 13½" high × 3" deep
(page 122)

Falling Leaves zipper pouch,
8½″ × 6¼″ (page 120)

Tulip-covered box with lid,
6¼″ diameter × 6¼″ high
(page 126)

Toaster key
holder, 3″ × 3″
(page 80)

Sewing Notions zipper pouch,
8″ wide × 4½″ high × 2½″ deep (page 99)

Morning Beverages mini quilt,
23˝ × 24½˝ (page 82)

Berry Stems tote,
10˝ wide × 11˝ high × 5½˝ deep
(page 124)

Cat Says, "Hi!" storage basket,
7″ wide × 6″ high × 5″ deep
(page 100)

Kitchen Shelf wall pocket,
10½˝ × 16½˝ (page 76)

Grandma's Sewing Machine
needlecase, 4½˝ × 5˝ (page 99)

On the Go key holder,
2½″ × 3½″ (page 84)

Strawberry Jam coaster,
8″ × 8″ (page 80)

Pears on the Vine zipper
pouch, 8½″ × 7″ (page 123)

Strawberry Bouquet basket,
7½˝ diameter × 7½˝ high
(page 86)

Pretty cover, 15″ × 13″, with Teaspoon and Teapot (page 79) and Sugar Jar and Tea Mug (page 78)

Love Letter zipper pouch,
10½˝ × 8˝ (page 88)

And just for fun, I thought I would show you two patterns made in quilting cottons, like the patterns in my books *Sew Illustrated—35 Charming Fabric & Thread Designs*, *Diary in Stitches*, and *Zakka from the Heart* (all by C&T Publishing).

Sew Happy mini quilt, 12″ × 12″, with quilting cotton appliqués (page 90). Also see Sewing Time Pocket Folder (page 36).

My Jam snack mat, 9½″ × 9½″, with quilting cotton appliqués (page 73)

STITCHES AND PATTERNS

See Downloadable Patterns (page 6) to download and print all the patterns.

MAMA'S KITCHEN

Baking Time

My Jam

See the project idea (page 71).

Best Utensils

See the project idea (page 55).

Kitchen Shelf

See the project idea (page 64).

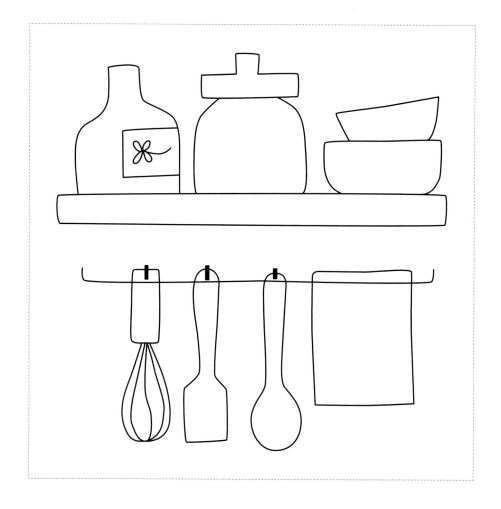

Try to mix fabrics for
additional charm.

Sugar Jar

See the project idea (page 69).

Tea Mug

See the project idea
(page 69).

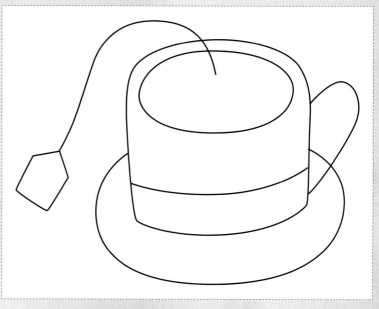

Teaspoon

See the project idea (page 69).

Teapot

See the project idea (page 69).

Toaster

See the project idea (page 59).

Strawberry Jam

See the project idea (page 66).

Breakfast

This pattern was used in Little Patch Coasters (page 14).

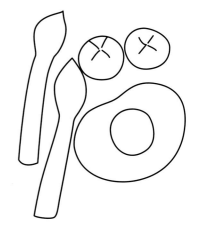

Egg Fry

This pattern was used in Little Patch Coasters (page 14).

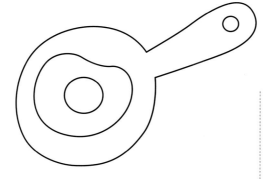

Mmm ... Marshmallows

This pattern was used in Little Patch Coasters (page 14).

A Place for You

See the project idea (page 56).

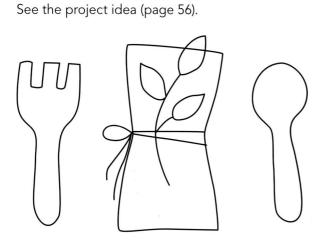

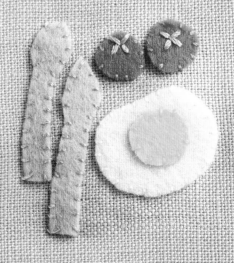

Morning Beverages

See the project idea (page 61).

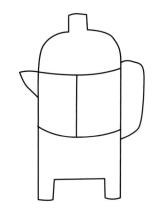

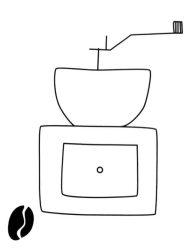

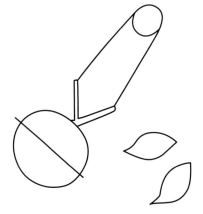

Mug of Love

Carafe

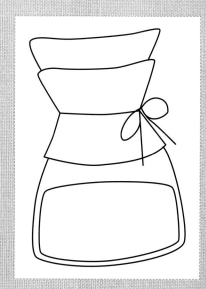

On the Go

See the project idea (page 66).

FRIENDSHIP

Picnic

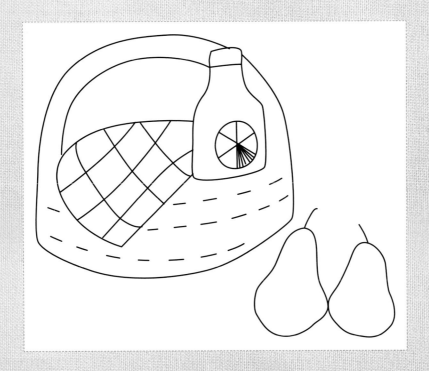

Strawberry Bouquet

See the project idea (page 68).

Love Letter

See the project idea (page 70).

Flowers for You

Pitcher Full of Flowers

CREATING

Sew Happy

This pattern was used for the front of Sewing Time Pocket Folder (page 36).
See the additional project idea (page 71).

Drawing Table

On My Desk

This pattern was used for the front of Pocket Pencil Case (page 20).

Sewing Day

This pattern was used for the front of Boxy Sewing Case (page 28).

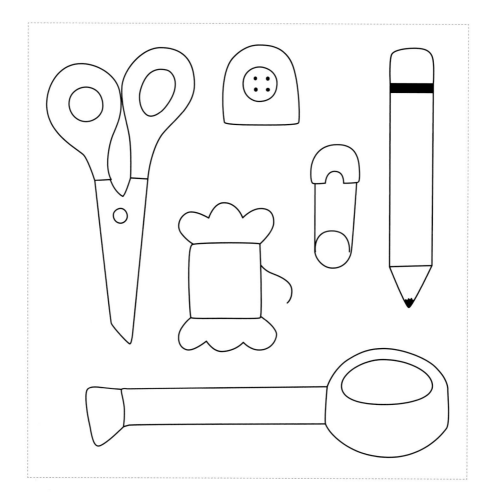

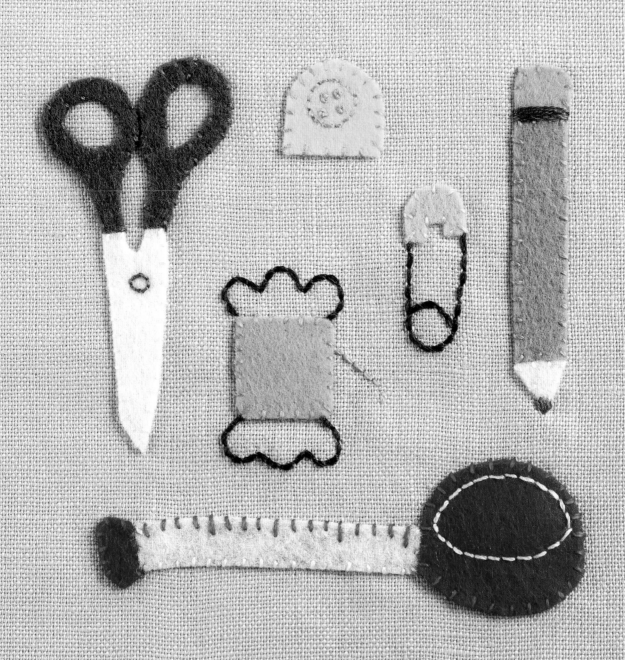

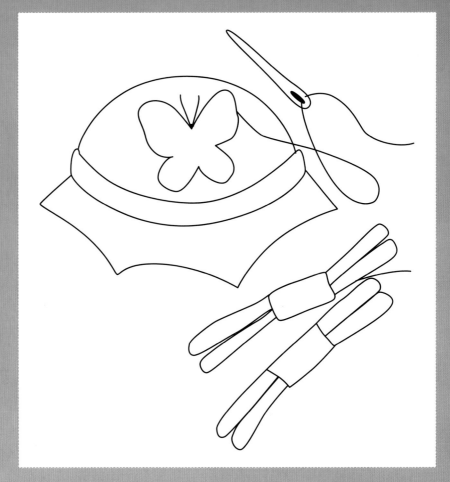

Happy
Stitching

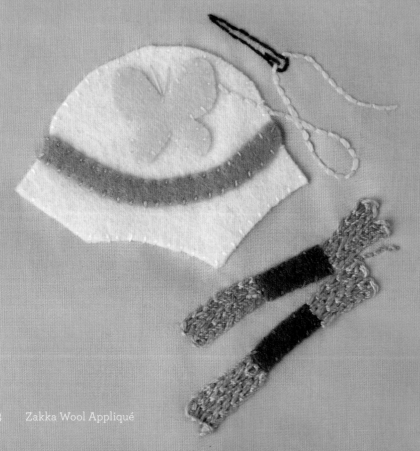

Grandma's Sewing Machine

See the project idea (page 65).

Sewing Notions

See the project idea (page 60).

 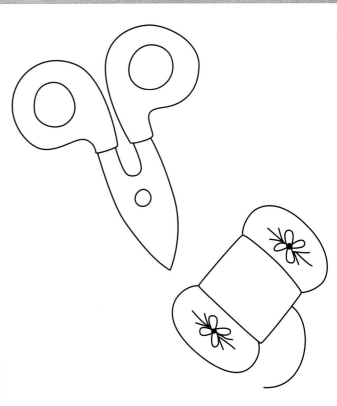

ANIMALS

Cat Says, "Hi!"

See the project idea (page 63).

Happy Fox

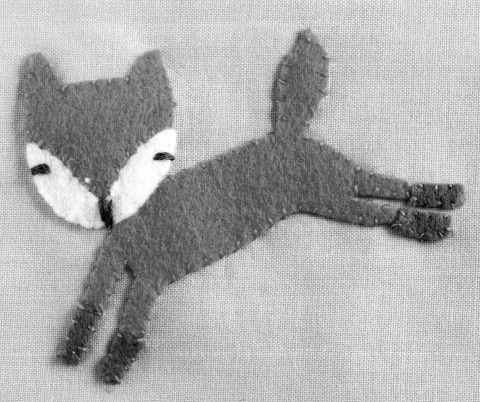

Winter Fox

Our Best Friends

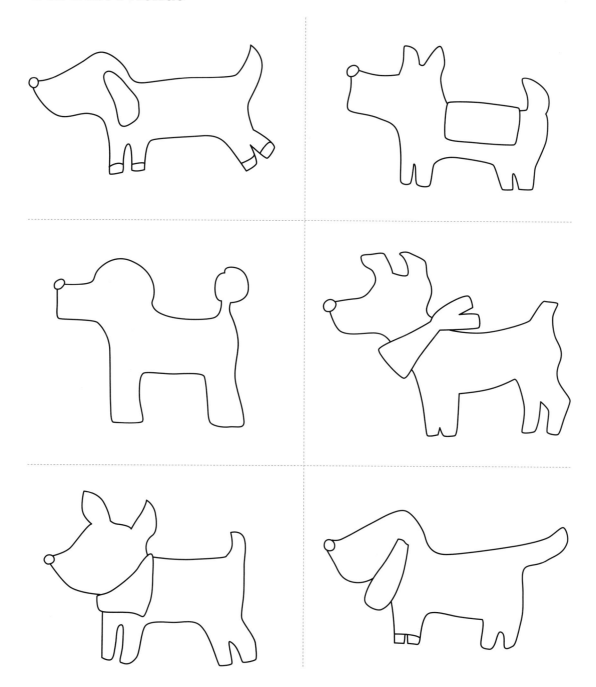

THE SEASONS

Spring

Summer

SUMMER

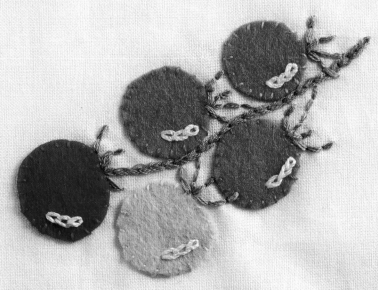

SUMMER

Autumn

AUTUMN

AUTUMN

Winter

WINTER

GARDENS

Blossom

See the project idea (page 54).

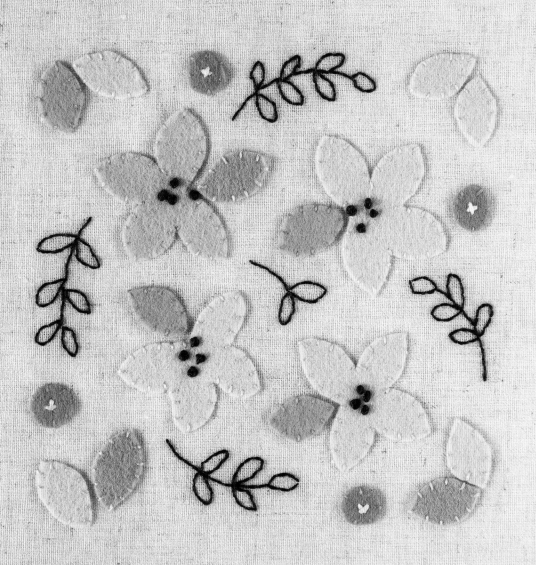

Dogwood in Bloom

This pattern was used for the front of Floral Handbag (page 48).

Summer Garden

Windblown Bouquet

This pattern was used for the front of Jardin Pillow (page 42).

New Blooms

Falling Leaves

See the project idea (page 58).

Floral Vine

See the project idea (page 57).

Pears on the Vine

See the project idea (page 67).

Berry Stems

See the project idea (page 62).

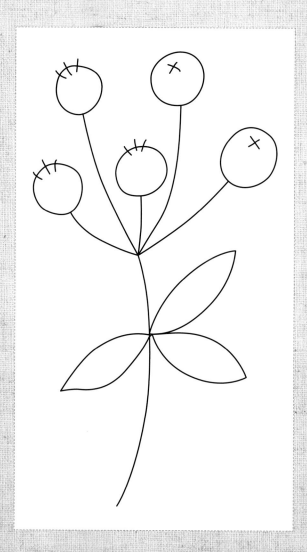

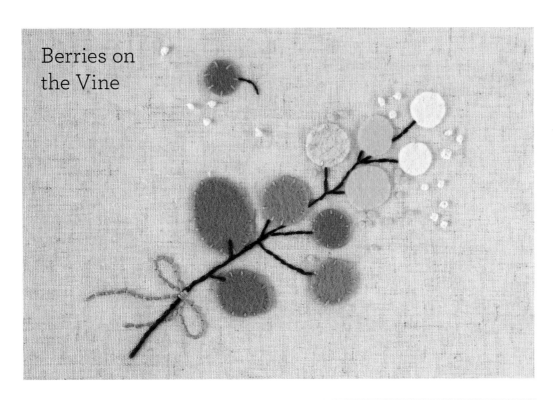

Berries on the Vine

Just Picked

Tulips

See the project idea (page 59).

About the Author

Minki Kim is a fabric and pattern designer with her own whimsical style. As a formally trained sculptor and self-taught sewist, she found that designing fabrics and creating art with fabric and thread were natural steps in her evolution as an artist.

Photo by Chloe Park

Minki discovered sewing as a creative outlet when her children were small. She wanted to capture the beauty of ordinary moments, first with hand embroidery and later recreating them with her sewing machine and fabric—literally drawing with thread. Capturing ordinary moments in beautiful sewing illustrations to make keepsake snapshots of daily life has become her signature style.

The author of *Sew Illustrated—35 Charming Fabric & Thread Designs*, *Diary in Stitches*, and *Zakka from the Heart* (all by C&T Publishing), Minki has also designed several fabric collections for Riley Blake Designs. She is originally from Korea but now calls Southern California home. She lives with her husband and three daughters.

Visit Minki online and follow on social media!

Blog: minkikim.com

Pattern shop: sewingillustration.com

Pinterest: /zeriano

Instagram: @zeriano

Also by Minki Kim:

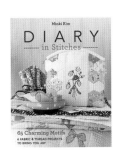

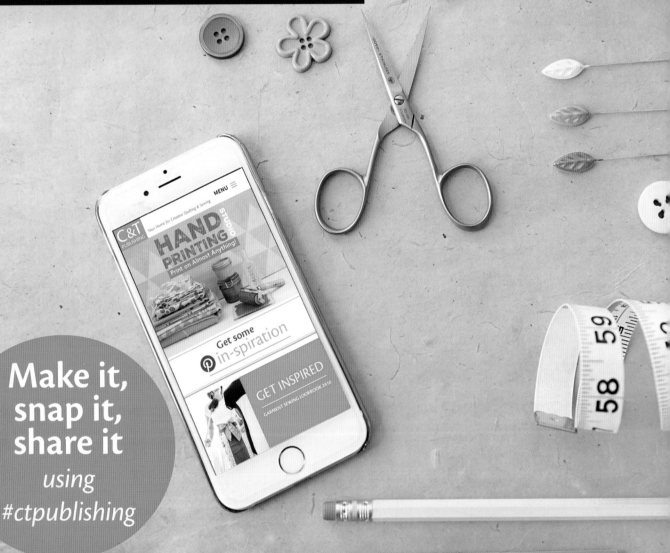

Want even more creative content?

Make it, snap it, share it *using #ctpublishing*